Rumination:

Overcome Your Destructive Thoughts and Start Thinking Positively

By Lana Otoya

Table Of Contents

FREE 10 Day Self Care Challenge

- Subscribe to my email list and get my 10 Day Self Care Challenge as a FREE bonus
- 10 Days of actionable tasks to help get you started on your self care journey.
- Download all 10 days in one PDF
- Clear your mind, feel happier
- Note: You'll receive notifications for when my next eBook goes on FREE promo
- https://millennialships.lpages.co/rumination-optin/

Note from the Author

Hey, thanks for grabbing a copy of my book! Before we continue, I thought it would be best if I introduce myself. My name is Lana and I am a relationship and self care blogger. I founded a blog called Millennialships.com which helps people strengthen themselves and their relationships in order to live a better life.

Everything I coach about, speak about and write about – yes including this book - is based on the Millennialships concept. Millennialships stands for Millennial + Relationships. The concept is simple and is as follows:

Better Yourself

Better Your Relationships

Better Life.

When I say better yourself, I am talking about taking care of your mental health and learning skills that will help you thrive in relationships. When you make people happy and people make you happy, it gives you purpose and you live a meaningful life.

Therefore it is *so important* for you to do everything in your power to keep your mental health up. It is the foundation upon which your whole life balances on top of. The fact that you picked up this book means that you take your mental health seriously and want to learn how to keep a healthy mind. If you continue to do this your whole life, you will go far my friend. Mental health techniques can be learned and shaped so that you can live your best life.

When you read the contents of this book, understand that there is no one size fits all solution. This book has multiple solutions and techniques and if something doesn't work, move on to the next suggestion and try that. I can assure you that you'll be left with a collection of techniques that work for you and you will be so glad you started learning how to train your brain.

Introduction

That inner voice inside your head. The one that *never stops*. The thoughts which invade your mind and take control of how you think and how you feel. They grab on tight and do not let go, repeating over and over destructive phrases and questions.

- "Why am I such a loser?"
- "I am so worthless."
- "I am just a burden."

You dwell on these thoughts, and they play in your head on a constant loop. No matter what you try, they are always there, and it seems as though you are falling deeper and deeper away from who you once were.

I cannot blame those for falling into negativity, for our world is in continuous peril. Our health, security, economy, and environment are all in a pit of uncertainty. Social media is both a worldly blessing and a curse. We can now connect with people all over the globe with the click of a button, but it leaves us feeling disconnected and alone. Void of real, deep and meaningful relationships.

Social media also has us comparing our lives to others. We overthink everything.

"Cindy" is getting married, "Jim" is going on vacation, "Laura" is eating a delicious meal in a fancy restaurant, *again.* One thing is for sure – the overthinking, comparing yourself and the *rumination* must stop. You deserve peace.

I am writing this book to help those grow from distress to find promise, opportunity, and renewal in their lives. Throughout this book, you will be shown the way to unshackle yourself from your current state of mind and see the world in a more positive light. You will never be asked to ignore your issues or become passive about your challenges. Instead, you will learn how to make deliberately meaningful choices that will lead you to be joyful and fulfilled in your life. You will also learn how to gain control over your brain and your thoughts and how they make you feel.

Who This Book Is For

If you feel burdened by your mind, then this book is a great starting point to gain your life back. Rumination is all about thinking the same things time and time again and worrying about the future and the past. If you find that your thoughts have turned to anxieties that keep you up at night and have survived through periods of depression, then it is time to take the weight of the world from your shoulders so that you can live a fruitful life.

No matter how heavy your rumination is, you are more than capable of amazing things, which also include feeling better, both inside and out. There is no judgment passed throughout this book as you learn to have a different relationship with your mind.

The information you will discover in this book is based on techniques from practitioners that have gone through thousands of years of testing and have withstood scrutiny from scientists. They have done all the hard work and research so that we can reap the benefits. And no worries, you don't need to be a Buddhist to benefit from the wise words you are about to read as you find a more mindful path.

It's time to make the choice to learn how to find a better path to a happier life!

Throughout the next chapters, we will focus on ways to help you overcome these destructive ways of thinking. As you read, remember that you are taking the step in the right direction. You know that these thoughts have only hindered your life and you are ready to take control and overcome.

Chapter 1: What Is Rumination?

Rumination is the psychological term for a deep focused thought. Many times, rumination is an effective way to find a solution to a problem. However, if the thoughts are left unchecked or negative in nature, they can ultimately harm a person's overall well-being.

The word rumination derives from the word 'ruminate,' which in Latin means to chew cud, a process in which cattle grind their food, swallow, regurgitate, and rechew their feed. In humans, so many of us ruminate over specific issues.

Ruminating over darkened thoughts is a sure-fire way to develop depression, anxiety, bipolar, and other mental disorders that seep into the deterioration of your mental health. It can impair your thinking capabilities and your ability to problem solve, which can drive away any social support you have in your life.

Now that we know exactly what rumination is, it helps us understand when and *why* we should put a stop to it.

Healthy Rumination is Solution Based

Let's dig a bit deeper. Healthy rumination is solution based. It's when you are going over a problem again and again in hopes of finding a positive outcome. For example, if you're building a house and are designing the floor plan, you might go over this floor plan again and again in your mind. You'll make adjustments, then visualize it again and then make more adjustments. This is still considered rumination but it moves *forward* towards a solution. This is healthy.

So how can we know that our rumination has slipped into the unhealthy zone?

If there is no possible solution for the thing we're ruminating about, the rumination is pointless.

Rumination with no solutions include but are not limited to:

- Events in the past
- Events in the future
- Things we cannot control
- Thoughts that are not *objectively* true

Going into these in more detail will help you see why rumination is an ineffective way to use your brain power.

Events in the past

Those of us who have been given the curse of destructive thinking tend to ruminate about past events. This could be serious things like past traumas, emotionally charged events (such as a fight with a partner) or little things like saying something embarrassing at a party. Although very different to the naked eye, the one thing these all have in common is that they have already happened.

Assuming that the event was not caught on video, once it is over, it no longer exists. It only exists in your mind and in the mind of anyone who is currently thinking about it.

When you relive a traumatic or negative experience in your mind, you bring it back to life and then it hurts you. Thinking about it only brings it back to life, it doesn't change what happened. It is for this reason that *past events* are a *no solution* rumination.

Now, before we move on I want to make it clear that we are talking about the past event itself. I know that past events can lead to *current* psychological issues (that's why PTSD is a thing) but right now we're simply breaking down the meaning of an event that is in the past which means it cannot be changed. Once we start discussing current emotional or mental states that have occurred as a result of a past event, we are actually talking about the present not the past.

Events in the Future

Events in the future is a tricky one because it *seems* like we can control the future, but we actually can't. We can help mold the future so that it is more likely to go the way we want but nothing can predict what is really going to happen. Let's use the example of a big exam.

If we're thinking and thinking about the exam because we're nervous about failing it, this will *not* change the outcome of the exam. Even if we studied all night, we could sleep in on the day of the exam, miss it and then fail it. The point here is that we only know the future once it turns into the present. This makes thinking about the future a *no solution* rumination.

A quick reminder here is that *rumination* is when you have the same thought over and over again. Thinking about your future, making plans and making goals are all healthy. It's only when you constantly worry and stress about the same topic without taking action, that it gets unhealthy.

For example, if you're constantly thinking "I can't pay the bills, I wonder how I'm going to pay the bills" without thinking of *solutions* to that problem then it becomes *no solution* rumination which is unhealthy.

14

Things That We Cannot Control

Anytime we think about something that we cannot directly control, we enter a *no solution* rumination. An excellent example of this one is ruminating about our weight.

But what about diet and exercise, we can control that can't we?

Yes, you can control your diet and exercise but you cannot control your weight. Your weight will be determined by your diet, exercise, environment, hormones, health, height, genes etc.

Since healthy rumination is solution based, it will serve you better to ruminate about your diet rather than your weight. You can tweak your diet at home, get someone to meal prep for you, see a nutritionist etc. There are many solutions that can result from ruminating about your diet but ruminating about your actual weight is *no solution* rumination.

Things That Are Not Objectively True

This category is referring to thoughts that you might think are true, but they are not factually true. Thoughts like this include:

- "I'm worthless"
- "Nobody likes me"
- "The world would be better without me"

All these thoughts are your opinion, they cannot be proven.

What's more accurate is the following:

- "I feel like I'm worthless"
- "I feel like nobody likes me"
- "I feel like the world would be better without me"

Now that we put "I feel" at the beginning, you can ask yourself – but why do I feel this way? Why do I feel like I'm worthless even though this is not a fact that can be proven and is likely untrue? Once you ask yourself that, now you can start thinking of reasons why you might feel this way and start solution based rumination.

If you find yourself slipping into *no solution* rumination, find out what you *can solve* and start ruminating about that – it will be a step in the right direction. Solution based rumination is not easy to do and will take some practice and learning so don't be discouraged if you're not the best at it right away, you will get better.

16

Why You're Stuck with Uncontrollable Overthinking:

Depressive rumination occurs mostly in females and is a direct reaction to sadness. In men, however, rumination occurs more when emotions are derived from angry feelings.

The reason we ruminate seems to be largely cultural. This is because what is okay for women versus men is emotionally different. However, those who ruminate share the same characteristics, such as:

- Perceiving that they face stressors, they are unable to control
- Having a past filled with trauma
- Believing that they are gaining some kind of insight from ruminating
- Showcasing characteristics of personality such as:
    - o Tendency to overvalue relationships with others in a way they believe they must sacrifice themselves to maintain them
    - o Perfectionism
    - o Neuroticism

Rumination, Anxiety, And Depression:

As you can imagine, ruminating is one of the clear

similarities between anxiety and depression, for it is repeatedly going over a problem or thought without completion. When you are depressed, themes that ruminate in your head are that you are worthless or inadequate in some way. The repetition of these feelings raises your levels of anxiety, which them interferes with solving issues. Therefore, your state of depression deepens further.

The way in which our brain functions plays an essential role in why we ruminate, the main one relating to memory. We recall things that are related to each other, thanks to the existence of neural networks. When we get a 'woe is me' attitude, this network lights up. It connects directly to other memories that made you feel this way, worsening your state of anxiety and/or depression.

Our natural brain chemistry makes it extremely difficult to switch to another, more positive perspective that allows us to find solutions to our issues. When we fail to problem-solve, our rumination deepens, which reinforces our anxious and depressing thoughts.

There are two main concepts to switch off the act of ruminating that you will take notice of within this book:

Concept 1: Separating Your Problems and Making Plans

Rumination is a big issue when it comes to solving problems that are creating obstacles in your life. It prevents you from moving forward in life and with adequate solutions. However, it is when we begin to unhook our issues from one another that you have a chance to see the problem for what it is and eliminate it entirely from your life.

There are many times that people are surprised to discover that they were never faced with a dilemma to begin with when they took off the blindfold of rumination.

For instance, let's talk about a man, we will call him Tim. He was anxious and depressed due to his work life, his debt, his angry colleagues, and the overwhelming number of hours he had to put into his work.

Tim knew what to do about his debt. However, he tangled it up with the issue of worrying about what others would think, believing the people in his life would be angry with him about how he eliminated that debt.

Tim then ruminates on what to say to his angered folks in his life, "*I wish I could walk away from them. If I could get caught up at work with those expense reports, I could look for another job.*"

Tim's debt issue has nothing to do with how he wanted to try to make everyone in his life happy or finding the time to find a new job. However, he managed to connect these unrelated issues together, which makes it almost impossible for him to let go of any of them.

What Tim should do are as follows:

- Make a list of issues and put them into separate columns
- Make a plan for the first issue in actionable steps
- Do the same thing for each issue you are ruminating over
- Look at the columns. Are any of those steps connected to one another?
- Does a problem not have a solution? Write down a time when you think you will have more information to help resolve it
- Now, when those issues come to mind, you can tell yourself that you have a plan!

Concept 2: Getting Yourself Out of The Negative Neural Network

To stop ruminating, you will need to stop focusing on the negative and perform actions that activate the network that will tell you that things will be alright. Your neural networks are turned on and off by your mood. This can be connected to other moods and feelings when you become afraid of a bad/unrealistic outcome.

Instead, choose to remember times when things worked out, even when you were scared of them. Networks triggered by anxiety can then be lead to ruminating over positive outcomes.

Things you can do to shift to a positive neural network:

- Talk to family and friends to help you recall positive times. Ensure the people you talk to are encouraging and positive themselves, or this will be counterintuitive
- Go over happy memories in your head. Recall what you felt like, not necessarily what your mind might have been thinking at the time. You will surprise at the happiness you felt through physical sensations.
- Music has the power to place you directly in the driver's seat of a positive recollection. Personally, many times I listen to songs that were popular in high school and college to remind me of the days before things became complicated in the world of

adulthood. It reminds me that everything happens for a reason.

- Visit and take a walk in locations that help you to enter a more positive frame of mind.

-

Understanding Rumination Through Worry:

To better understand rumination, we'll need to discuss the concept of worry. We've all worried about something in our life. Be it a job interview, financial issues, or worrying about the well-being of family members. These thoughts cause us to focus on the what-ifs, such as:

- "What if I don't get this job?"
- "What if I don't have enough money to pay my bills?"

Most of the time, we try to work through these thoughts and find a solution. But there are some that just dwell on the matter. Once we make the decision to dwell, those thoughts start to spiral out of control. We are left worrying and fearful of everything with no clear solution in our sight. This is the beginnings of the process of rumination.

A person does not wake up one morning with overwhelming thoughts, but they slowly build up to this point over a period of time. The thought starts as a seed, and once that seed is watered with doubt or fear, it begins to grow with its vine snaking through your subconscious and slowly taking over and controlling your very outlook on life.

Rumination not only affects the way you think but also your emotions. When we dwell on a thought, our body reacts with the physical representation of the emotion.

For instance, if there was a time in your life when you were rejected, it could have been rejection been by a person or a loss of job opportunity. Rumination causes a person to focus on those rejected feelings and play them over and over again within their mind. When someone is rejected, they might feel hurt or angered that someone would look past all the valuable assets they had to offer.

Focusing on those emotions will cause your heart to race, your breathing to intensify, and a pit to form in your chest. You relive the rejection. This way of thinking is not productive or helpful. What these thoughts try to do is make you feel helpless, lonely, and worthless, so you are unable to make a positive change in your life. Remember, a past event no longer exists unless you're thinking about it.

Ridding Oneself of Rumination

Those that ruminate over their thoughts on a daily basis find it challenging to divert their negative train of thought. Studies have shown that simple distraction has drastically decreased the time that these folks over-contemplate their thoughts and feelings. It helps to mitigate their tendency to focus on problems and blame themselves as well.

As you flip through the following chapters, we will be discussing many strategies. We shall also treat some easy to learn techniques that you as a ruminator or those you know that dwell on the negative can use in their everyday lives, such as:

- The importance of small steps/actions in beginning to solve issues
- Reassessing perceptions that are negative, such as high expectations of people in your life
- Getting rid of unattainable and/or unhealthy goals and developing sources to rebuild self-esteem and self-confidence
- Exercises that will help you to establish a more stable peace of mind
- Ways to integrate a healthier daily routine for success and positivity
- Strategies that can be used at the drop of a hat to redirect negative thoughts

Chapter 2: How Anxiety and Negativity Can Overtake Your Life

Let's face it, almost every single human being on this planet falls into the depths of hardships and into the darkness of anxiety, depression, and other negative ailments. During these times in our lives, we second guess ourselves and those that surround you, always think of ill thoughts about the future, etc.

Those that live day in and day with anxious thoughts and feelings, go through panic attacks on a regular basis or have a phobia of some kind feel ashamed of their "sickness." It has the tendency to make people feel insane, even though they truly aren't. Just like with all people, some days are better than others, but those who experience symptoms caused by these mental ailments have a higher count of bad than good days.

They often feel that they are always under a dark cloud that pours rain, but that rain is not made up of just water. Those drops from the sky above their head are created from startling visions. Other sources are disturbing logic, feelings of worthlessness and/or hopelessness and look that they receive from both loved ones and strangers. This is more pathetic when they truly believe they are in a type of personal crisis or feel as if they are about to be pushed over the edge. This is just a small portion of what it is like to live with anxiety, something I used to struggle with a lot, before I learned tips and tricks on how to overcome it.

What Is Anxiety?

Especially for those that have either been recently diagnosed with being plagued by anxiety or have had it but have never taken the time to get to understand it, it is pretty crucial to gain a deeper knowledge as to how it functions within our bodies and minds.

Anxiety, described at its simplest, is our bodily reaction to unfamiliar or dangerous environments and scenarios. Everyone has the tendency to get anxious from time to time and feel distressed or uneasy. This happens perhaps before a big game, performing in front of an audience or right before a huge job interview.

Feeling anxious is a natural response that our bodies can feel during moments like these. Anxiety gives us the boost we need to be consciously aware and alert to prepare us for certain situations. Our body's "fight-or-flight" response is under this umbrella of reactions. But imagine feeling like this ALL the time, even during the calmest of moments? Picture a life where you have issues concentrating on everyday tasks, where you may be frightened to leave the safety of your home when you cannot fall or stay asleep because your mind is in a constant whirlwind of thought? Living with an anxiety disorder is debilitating. That is putting it lightly in some cases.

But what if I told you that there were simple strategies that when practiced and implemented into everyday life, that you could rid yourself of feeling this way? Even better, we are all capable of learning these techniques and putting them into everyday use!

Likely Causes of Anxiety and Depression:

Each one of us is unique, and that goes for how certain disorders resonate within us and as to why we are undergoing their torment as well. There typically are several factors that cause anxiety disorders to plant themselves in our mind and grow. Some influences may be:

- Chemistry of the brain
- Life events
- How we grew up
- Environmental factors
- Genetics
- Side effect to particular medications
- Occurrence of other mental health issues
- Alcohol, prescription medication or drug abuse
- Physical, emotional or mental trauma
- History of anxiety that runs in family bloodlines

- Stress that lasts an extended period of time
- Chemical imbalances in the body and/or brain

The feelings and thoughts that anxiety promotes within a sufferer create a bubble that makes one feel alone. So, it may be surprising to some that anxiety disorders are the most common of mental illnesses with the U.S. Over 40 million American adults are living with one of these disorders every day. If it is any consolation, you are by no means alone when it comes to feeling the way you do. There is still a lot of research being put into finding out why anxiety plagues so many individuals, its specific causes and why it resonates within individuals in such vast ways.

When it comes down to thriving with an anxiety disorder, you must recognize what sets off the symptoms that agonize you and find ways, no matter how unique or used, to relieve yourself of them. This is much easier said than done. Some people never really know what upsets their anxiety, while others can pinpoint certain things and avoid them at all costs. Triggers can be almost anything and are fueled by specific events that have happened in the past or are set off by a combination of different things. Some types of triggers are set off by:

- Physical or emotional distress
- Stressful situations
- Work-related stress
- School-related stress
- Relationships and/or friendships
- Illness
- Ways the mind processes life and situations that arise

For some, anxiety attacks feel like they literally come from the sky and typically like to hit you when you least expect it and the most inconvenient times. This uncertainty alone can cause one to feel anxious, which is why having the ability to see your triggers before they sprout and quickly grow is crucial. Having the power to identify what triggers your symptoms of anxiety can prepare you for possible scenarios where they are likely to reside. It can also help you in developing effective coping skills to deal with your anxiety when it is sprung upon you.

The best news in all of this is that anxiety and depression are treatable, but not exactly in the way that your mind just turned to. Yes, there are things such as therapy sessions, prescribed medications, and holistic approaches to relieving their anxiety-driven symptoms. However, a huge part of the reason that huge portions of our society feel so crummy about their lives is that their minds have yet to be trained to see the positive. They are not mindful in the way they are living, resulting in that inevitable 'lost' feeling. Throughout the next few chapters, you will hopefully be inspired by the many benefits that will accrue when you turn your method of thinking around and the strategies to get yourself in a much healthier state of mind.

Chapter 3: An Introduction to Positive Thinking

I am sure you have heard someone tell you to, *"Look on the bright side!"* or *"View your glass as half full, not half empty."* When I heard these sayings, I would typically roll my eyes, sigh heavily, and walk away. But science is constantly finding new evidence that links being more optimistic with major benefits on both the mind and body.

So it's not that the "look at the bright side" advice is wrong, it's just that it's a lot easier said than done. It is important to understand this because then you can see that "looking on the bright side" is actually the goal, but we have to learn techniques and practice them in order to reach that goal.

Next time someone says "just look at the glass half full", the answer you should tell yourself is "I'm working on it". If you constantly work at thinking positively, you will start doing it more often and the unhealthy rumination will lessen.

The Path of Least Resistance

When you are depressed or anxious, the thought of "thinking positively" feels like the devil is inviting you to the depths of hell. You want to reject it and push it away *so bad*. Why is it that your mind is rejecting something that you *know* is probably good for you?

The answer is, *the path of least resistance.*

Your consciousness is made up of thought patterns, habits and routines. This means that you'll often think about the same types of things on a regular basis – whether these are positive or negative.

Whatever your mind chooses to think about *most of the time* is going to be its path of least resistance. It's going to be the thing that is the easiest to think about.

When I was suffering from a lot of anxiety and stress from my job, I was *always* thinking about work. Even if I was enjoying a lovely dinner on the patio or watching my favorite TV show, my brain would casually drift off to thinking about work and then I would feel anxious and stressed about it.

The reason my brain would do this was because it was so used to going there. It was simply a routine that I had created and it became my path of least resistance.

Your path of least resistance should be a positive place.

The Roads of Brain City

Let's pretend your brain is a city, we'll call it Brain City. In your city, you have positive buildings (aka positive thoughts) and negative buildings (negative thoughts). Every single time you think negatively, you build a road to a negative building. Every time you think positively, you build a road to a positive building.

If you're always thinking about negative things, the roads leading to your negative buildings will be nicely paved highways with no speed limit. They will be your paths of least resistance. So if you start the day with a little tiny negative thought (i.e. It's so cold and rainy today) then you are right on the highspeed freeway to the negative building. Just one little thought was enough to get you going 200 Mph down negative road to the negative building and put you in a negative mindset for the rest of the day.

Then, someone like me (hello!) comes a long and says "you should think positively" which means, you should go to a positive building in Brain City. You'll think about that for a moment and then realize... the roads to the positive buildings are no good! They are unpaved dirt roads that are windy and uphill. They are the path of maximum resistance because you haven't spent any time building those roads.

If you are depressed, anxious or suffer from rumination, your roads to positive buildings are not fun to drive on and when you drive on them, it won't be easy. You have a lot of work to do to build those positive roads, but once you get them all built up – your negative roads won't be so tempting.

Now that you understand this concept, it will be a lot easier for you to start building the positive roads. The rest of the chapters in this book will be suggestions and techniques for some of the easiest ways to start building positive roads.

If you try meditating and it doesn't work right away, that doesn't mean it's not working. Maybe you've been meditating for one week and you think "this isn't working" but what you don't realize is that you have flattened the dirt and started pouring concrete on a positive road. The road might not be ready to drive on just yet but you're starting to build it.

Before we go into those techniques, I want to hammer home the point that positivity is a goal you should be aiming for. There are countless benefits of positivity to your overall health, here are a few.

Benefits of Positivity on Your Body

Longer Life

Being more optimistic can decrease the rate at which you age, which prolongs your lifespan. When you think in a positive light, you are much less likely to die from serious health issues. Pessimism feeds stress, which can make you sick and develop ailments such as heart disease, just to name one.

Makes for Stronger Immune Health

If you hate being sick, then positive thinking is not only a much cheaper alternative to over-the-counter medications. However, it is a natural remedy that works better than most drugs. If you are a constant Negative Nancy, you are much more likely to get sicknesses like the cold and flu, since negativity weakens essential areas of the brain that help with immune responses.

Benefits of Positivity on the Mind

It Fights Off Depression

Psychologists have found that depression is strongly linked to a negative mindset. When one is able to simply change their point of view to see the positive rather than focus on the pessimistic aspects of what they are going through, they are able to fight against the development of depression as much as 54% more. Positivity improves mood, no matter the situation at hand and is better at treating depression than almost all other therapies.

Stronger Sense of Confidence

Positive thinkers are naturally more confident. I mean, they do not want to spend the time pretending they are in the shoes of another person. They want to strive to love themselves the way they are.

It Is Easier to Accomplish Success

Optimistic individuals are better able to focus on the good they do rather than their failures. They see failures as not short-comings but as golden opportunities to learn and grow. They are always open-minded to try out new things and embracing different methods of thinking. This is one of the essential parts of leading a fruitful life.

Stronger Motivation

Having a positive attitude helps to fuel your motivation levels and help you start on what you wish to achieve. You will find that having an optimistic attitude gets you to where you want to go much faster and easier than dwelling in the negative.

Resilience

When faced with an issue, positive thinkers are able to do whatever it takes to fix the problem and are not hesitant to ask for the assistance of other people. Extremely negative situations, such as a natural disaster may arise. Research has found that having positive emotions encourages groups of people to thrive and provide leverage for one another to ensure survival.

Resilience is something that can be cultivated when you nurture positive thoughts and emotions, especially when it comes to facing terrible events. Positivity plays a huge role in maintaining stress, eliminating depression, and building up the coping skills needed to survive and serve in the future.

Chapter 4: Visualization Strategies to Keep Rumination at Bay

So now that we have discussed the benefits of thinking positively, how exactly can we start doing it?

The first step is visualization. When it comes to the terms of visualization, one should adopt the "seeing is believing" attitude. I like to refer to visualization techniques as a "mental vacation away from the everyday." With the methods and practices behind visualization itself, you can literally view the best of life, right from your own couch.

Grasp the Life You Want with Visualization

Visualization methods have been successfully practiced as ways to get yourself ahead in the game of life. Visualization is the best and cheapest intellectual way of gaining a connection between what you imagine that you want and going out and achieving it.

For people who suffer from the torment of anxiety's symptoms, the means of visualization give those a type of mental vacation from the world that plagues them. For those that have a severe anxiety disorder, being able to imagine much of anything besides negative activities is rather difficult. This is when real pictures come into play during practice, such as a poster of a serene and peaceful place, for the patient to imagine in their minds.

Guided Imagery: The Best and Most Popular Method of Visualization

Guided imagery is so universally accepted because we are already aware of the components that make them up:

Mind-Body Connection:

Our minds invent images that seem as realistic as if we were currently living them externally. During this process, our bodies do not quite understand the difference, which is why imagery seems so real.

For example, when we look at photos and read a potential recipe, our mouths start to salivate. Our minds equally imagine what that meal would taste and smell like, as well as how it would appear differently from the photo in your cookbook if you made it yourself. Our appetite then turns on.

The mind has a way of sending hints to our bodies. This goes for any type of imagery and senses that are associated with strong emotional elements. These kinds of sensory images are a strong language within our bodies that we are usually unaware of because they occur so naturally.

The Altered State:

The human body is gifted with the process of intense performance, rapid healing and powerful learning. When our minds are in this state, the brainwave activity, and chemistry shift, making us into more creative and intuitive people.

I'm sure you have missed a turn or exit while driving a time or two. This is because your mind is focused on something other than just driving. It is still aware of its surroundings, but we are also in a deepened state of thought when things like this occur. Our sensitivities to whatever is plaguing our minds at the time are raised, and our awareness of what is happening around us is decreased.

When we lose track of time or are looking directly at a person but do not absorb anything they are saying, this is another example of this type of daily phenomenon. Being within an altered state of mind is the manpower that is right behind the act of guided imagery. Think about the possibilities when we consciously decide to use altered states?

Locus of Control:

The last principle is known as the sense of being in control.

It makes one feel better and confident which helps us to achieve better results. The phrase *"locus in control"* is a medical term used to describe this feeling.

As human beings, when we recognize that we are in control of a situation, we have a naturally higher self-esteem. This yields us to better tolerate things such as stress and pain. When we feel good about ourselves, we perform optimally, whereas feeling hopeless or unworthy leaves us to perform poorly, as our confidence is lowered and the ability to cope effectively is just not there. The golden part of guided imagery is the fact that it is all internally guided by us. We can make the decision to even use locus of control. We can utilize it however we wish.

With these principles combined, our minds have the power to create multi-sensory images that trick our bodies into thinking are real. It is effective because it gives us a sense of control that we may otherwise not have. Next, we will discuss the different types of guided imagery techniques.

Guided Imagery Strategies

The following are some guided imagery strategies that can help you visualize. Not all of these strategies will work for everyone so it's best to write down your favorite one and give that a shot first to see if it helps. I recommend using these strategies in the morning after you wake up so that it will set the tone for a positive day.

Spiritual Imagery:

If you are religious or spiritual in any way, this technique will be excellent for you. Spiritual imagery induces a bigger picture of transcendent kinds of thoughts and feelings which are stimulated by conscious prayer. Sensing help from a higher power, such as animals, nature, or religion can help create a sense of connectivity with things that open the heart.

Psychological Imagery:

Psychological imagery takes note of someone's psychological problems by giving emotional information that helps them correct the core of this issue. For example, imagining loved ones surrounding you or seeing yourself through a loved one's eyes.

Metaphoric Imagery:

Metaphoric imagery is best used with symbols rather than reality. For example, watching a flower grow and open its petals is a direct metaphor that it has the potential to blossom again. Go on YouTube and search for a time lapse that could symbolize rebirth such as a sunrise or caterpillar turning into a butterfly. Imagine your old mental state dying and a new one being born.

End State Imagery:

End state imagery is utilized if one wishes to imagine an outcome or potential goal realistically. For example, picturing yourself strong and illness free, or playing a sport you wish to play someday. This is also referred to as mental rehearsal.

Feeling State Imagery:

Feeling state imagery has the power to change your mood and typically involves picturing yourself in a favorite place or looking back to a happy memory. Any types of images that reflect feelings of gratitude, safety and/or love, etc. are great qualifiers.

How to Use Guided Imagery

When it comes to visualization and diminishing rumination, practice makes perfect. Having someone you trust, or a recording as a guide will help you as a beginner master the ways of guided imagery. Be patient with yourself, it will take dedicated time and practice to really nail it down. Below are the simple steps to guided imagery:

Step 1: Get into a comfortable state of relaxation

This is a very crucial step if you wish to guide yourself into a session with success. The more relaxed you are, the better the results:

- Take time to allow your body to become limp in stature.
- Release the tensions that you harbor within you that you picked up throughout the course of the day.
- Relax your muscles. Work your way from the top of your head all the way down your body to the end of your toes.
- Consciously relax and release the tensions you hold within you.

Step 2: Calm your mind

Now that you have gotten your body into a peaceful state of relaxation, it is not to turn down the minds grinding gears. You want your mind to be completely calm to achieve guided imagery. You want your thoughts processes to be free to fly from continuous thoughts. As a beginner, your mind will be jumping like a frog from one thought to the next. This is natural, for our minds perform this way subconsciously without any logic behind it. It is not used to the act of letting go. Learn to free yourself from all that

44

internal wording.

Step 3: Focus on your breathing

Take in nice, slow, and deep breaths of air, but do not make strain yourself. Make sure you are breathing with a sense of peace. You will feel your body become more relaxed with each of these breaths. When you consciously think about your breathing cycle, you are taking the action in calming your mind from its tendency to rapidly dwell on current life issues or situations. Breathing exercises occupy the mind just enough to have those issues temporarily disappear.

Step 4: Get into a meditative state

This goes for both your physical being and mental state of mind. Let yourself dive deeper into a state of calmness. You need to focus on making it to that destination of internal peace and comfort and dwell only in that destination. This is where you can connect to your inner spirituality. Once you have mastered guided imagery to this point, you will be profoundly taken aback by how heavenly this state really is.

Step 5: Project desired imagery

Once you have landed in a relaxed state, it is time to let your mind's creativity flow and spew images of what you wish to visualize. It may be things you want to accomplish or simple, happy thoughts. Once you have practiced this a time or two, your mind can easily paint images for you once you reach a state of peacefulness. You have the power to add in any components you wish to view. *You are the master of your own imagery.*

When using guided visualization...

When undergoing guided mastery, you will learn that picking specific components to add to your peaceful thoughts give you the best results. When you think of the distinguishing factors of a goal that you wish to achieve or add in definitive memories from a happy time, your brain has more of an ability to let it manifest in your mind and highly develop all your senses for a better session.

There are many recorded CD's, YouTube videos, and other media that you can test out at the beginning when you are first learning how to get yourself to that content and peaceful state of mind. Guided imagery skips much of the learning curves that are required by other means of visualization or meditation. Once you find one that suits you, really practice following the voice of the narrator, the way their voice changes throughout the session, what they are instructing you to do, etc. It takes the stress out of acquiring all that knowledge to hone this type of skill set to get your mind and body to your own mental reality.

Chapter 5: Meditation Techniques to Fight Rumination

There have been thousands of studies regarding the research of how the methods of meditation can help keep symptoms of rumination at bay. A great way to cope with negative thoughts is through meditation. Within this chapter, we will discuss how meditation alleviates rumination symptoms that can lead to anxiety, depression, and negativity.

Let's put rumination under the microscope. Why is it that we as a human race are so anxious? A common answer to this question relates to the theory of evolution. Back in our cave man days, anxiety would have been advantageous to our survival because our lives were constantly being threatened by our environment. Big storms, tigers, lack of food etc.

Back then, you didn't always have time to rationalize or think logically. You couldn't say "hm there's a tiger coming towards me, should I run?" If you did you'd be the tiger's dinner. So, people who stayed on their toes, looked out for danger and acted quickly without thinking were the ones that survived. Anxiety gave you an advantage.

Alas, our world has greatly changed since then. We no longer need to worry about *merely* surviving. We now want to live meaningful and happy lives. In today's world your anxiety is hurting you rather than saving your life.

Most of us think about the future rather than spending quality time *living* in the *present*. We also tend to dwell a lot on the past, thinking back as to how we could have done things differently and then what our lives would be like today.

There are other factors too, such as advancements in technology that can cause harm when overused or utilized in improper manners. We now have the ability to see what others think about us. We know too much of what goes on within the lives of other people. We are a race that does not know how to unplug to save our souls.

The means of meditation is not used to erase your negative thoughts but to help you to come back, be mindful of the present, and enjoy your present-day life.

Rumination and its negative effects are reduced with meditation because we are teaching ourselves to look at our world in the present in positive detail and take in all its glory, instead of dwelling in the future or the past. Instead of *thinking* about your life, you start to *live* it.

When it comes to meditation methods, you learn to bring your foggy focus back to the present. This provides you with a clearer and more stable state of mind. Meditation also allows us to quiet our brains, especially during times when it is overworked and overactive. Rumination fuels itself from the fact that we tend to be quite gullible when it comes to how we think and feel about things. Instead of looking deeper, we take things at face value, which can make us feel overwhelmed. Our anxious minds are always deluding our thoughts with "what-ifs."

Meditation fights against the way society have taught our brains to operate. It allows us to get off that over-active hamster wheel in our head, take a breath, and gain perspective in what to do next.

What Rumination Does to Our Bodies

Our mind and bodies are directly intertwined with one another, so it is no secret that having an overly anxious state of mind on an everyday basis is not good for neither your mental or physical well-being. Bodily effects of anxiety can include:

- Digestive and stomach issues

- Always feeling like you cannot quite catch your breath
- Twitching or shaking
- Trembling
- Inability to be able to relax
- Headaches
- Muscles tension
- Irritability and mood swings
- Fatigue
- Easily startled
- Insomnia

Sadly, these are just a few of the negative effects that rumination causes but meditation has the ability to turn these things around.

How Meditation Transforms the Brain

There is plenty of research that displays the correlation between the practice of meditation and the positive effects it has on the way our brain functions. Utilizing daily meditation methods has been shown to drastically change the grey matter that our brains are made up of.

Mediation has the power to greatly reduce anxiety

Meditation causes a domino effect in the brain that triggers the release of feel-good hormones such as dopamine, making it an effective treatment for anxiety and depression.

Improves attention and ability to concentrate

Meditation itself takes a large amount of intense concentration, and this can aid in the rise of cognitive abilities once it is practiced for a period of time.

Changes areas of the brain positively

The practice of meditation can cause our brains, even as adults, to warp and change in very positive ways. Practicing focused meditation increases the thickness of the hippocampus, which is the portion of our brain that is in charge of how we learn and retain memory.

This also goes for the parts of the brain that we use to regulate ourselves emotionally. And even better news is that with the thickening and growing of the more positive areas is the decrease in areas such as the amygdala, which is the part of our brains that triggers fear and rumination.

Reduces stress

Stress at too high of levels is a component that fuels us in feeling agitated and moody. Meditation allows individuals to take charge of how their mind and bodies react to changes that impact your emotional state of mind as well as important areas of the body such as the nervous system. Meditation allows those that practice it to effectively regular emotion.

Practicing Mindfulness

Mindfulness is a form of meditation that allows us to stop, take a breath, and truly take in the beauty of the everyday. Overall, it is respecting and being grateful that you are *alive* and well. In today's hectic world, we have to remind ourselves to take these crucial moments and really dive deep into how we really feel, both mentally and physically. Here are a few simple tips that anyone can add to their daily routine to start practicing the positive act of mindfulness.

Free yourself from the past and future

The first step to being mindful is to free yourself from the past and future. The past and the future are often *no solution* rumination topics. We live the majority of our present lives dwelling on what we could have done differently in our pasts and what we need to do in order to achieve the future we desire. We take very little time really experiencing our lives in the present, mindfulness will help ground us in the present.

Watch your thoughts

It is important to remember that mindfulness does not erase these thoughts, but it is rather about changing your mindset about them. This is why activities such as yoga or walking are paired with mindfulness meditation sessions. This pairing gives our minds a little something more to feed off of when clearing our thoughts and taking in our surroundings.

Try out new things

Taking the initiative to create changes in your normal routine and environment can do one a lot of good! Sit somewhere new during your lunch break. Get up a little earlier to get ready for the day. Go out and try a new activity or develop a new hobby. There are always new things to experience and explore. If your mind is intrigued by learning new, valuable and/or constructive things, it has little time to dwell on cloudier thoughts and feelings.

Choose the same time each day to meditate

For those with busy schedules, it is important to pick a regular time each day to practice mindfulness and conduct meditation sessions. This could be during your morning workout or walk, during a break at work or in the evening a few hours before bedtime.

Make sure that you stick to almost the same time every day, for then practicing mindfulness seems like less of a chore and more of a part of your everyday routine that you stick with to stay at your healthiest.

Take notice of the environment

Even when we are going merely about our busy lives, we still tend to notice small things. This includes how things taste, how the breeze feels on our skin, noticing people as they walk by, etc.

We have to learn how to consciously engage ourselves directly in our environment. This will help is dive deeper into ourselves, as well as hopefully help us bury our many anxious and/or depressive thoughts and feelings.

Easy Ways to Implement Mindfulness

As a human in today's world, we are almost all guilty of never taking enough time for ourselves. This makes us lose our connections to our inner selves, mind, and heart. Your inner being is constantly fighting against the outer world to get your attention. Here are a few strategies that you can incorporate into your regular schedule starting *today:*

Do your best to end the day positively

Before your head hits your pillow, take a moment to think back about the contents of your day. Otherwise, make it a habit of jotting things down that you appreciated and enjoyed. Learn how to be thankful for *everything*.

This will help in extinguishing those irritated moods that can overshadow the current day as well as the next. Stress breeds more stress. Take the time to think over, identify, and analyze the bad moments that may have happened throughout the day. This will help in looking for positive solutions to issues in the future.

Erase distracting thoughts

Think of thoughts as guests in a hotel that come and go. This means you should do your best to keep the pesky guests that want to stay awhile out. Your thoughts do not make up *who* you are. That's why with rumination, it is important to learn how to ground yourself and constructively sort through your thoughts and feelings.

You and only you have the power to bring yourself up and tear yourself down. You cannot stop those negative thoughts from knocking at your mind's door and peaking their ugly head inside, but you can keep them from entering your mind and taking it over.

Keep an everyday journal that you can write down how you truly feel about experiences, people and other such things in. For some people, writing this sort of stuff out helps them rid their minds of those thoughts because they are now on paper and not just trapped with the recesses of their mind.

Patience

There are moments throughout the day that calls for us to wait patiently. It can be waiting in the drive-thru for a meal, stopping at a red light, waiting for someone outside, etc. If you experience irritation in having to wait, it is an important tool to learn how to change your focus target.

Calm yourself down by searching for and concentrating on the things that surround you at that moment. If this does not work well for you, focus on your breathing patterns.

Baby steps

No matter how many tiny steps you take towards achievements or completing tasks, each step is still a step in the right direction. It is crucial to remember that quality always triumphs over quantity.

Take moments out of your day to break away from tasks. Mix up your schedule by planning vacations to get away from the everyday. Learn to celebrate small achievements in ways that suit you best. There are no shortcuts that people can successfully ride through life. Slow and steady usually wins the race.

It's ok to have flaws

Every single person on this planet has at least one weakness. No one is perfect no matter how hard they try. We live in a society where people kill themselves in striving for perfection. Ultimately, it is the imperfections that really mean something. It takes courage to admit our faults and shortcomings, but when we finally do, we can become better people. When we recognize our weaknesses, it only leaves room for improvement! We all make mistakes. It is how we learn and grow from them that showcase who we truly are.

Take a break from your phone

When we wake up, the first thing we do before we even have our chance to open our eyes is reach for our phones and look at our notifications to see if we "missed anything" or "who liked our posts." STOP this habit. Instead of waking up to a phone in your hand, use this time to build a healthy morning routine that gives you a positive start to the day.

Practice mindful eating

In the hustle and bustle of our daily lives, we tend to scarf down meals while we are hurrying off to a meeting or picking up the kids from activities. Make time to enjoy your food wholeheartedly. It is important to chew your food properly. This assists in your body properly breaking them down for digestion. It also communicates effectively with your stomach so that it knows when it is really full. If we shove food in our face, we eat fast and fill our stomachs with more food than we probably need.

Accept things as they are

We all wish that certain things could be different. There is not one single person who is 100% satisfied with everything in their life. Mindful people do not judge, and they accept things not at face value, but for what they are truly worth.

It is important to not mentally label things as "good" or "bad." Do not change your personality to adhere to other people's opinions. Learn to fill your life with individuals who have faith in you, who will be loyal to you and that you trust. Do not try to warp things simply because you cannot accept them.

Rid yourself of jealousy

This might be the hardest one on the list. We can't help but look at other people's lives and see that the grass is greener. The best thing you can do for your mental health is to stop feeling jealous if someone achieves something or gets something that you want.

Instead, feel happy for them and know that they are only human. If they got that thing, you can get it too. Use them as motivation to realize that getting what you want is possible. Whether this is a romantic partner, great job, salary increase or a beautiful home – if they have it, you can get it too. Be happy for them and support others so that they will do the same for you.

My favorite mini-meditation technique

This is a great technique you can use to gain control over your thoughts. The more you use it, the better you will get at knowing when you need to perform it.

- Step 1: Look around and take note of where you are

- Step 2: Close your eyes, notice the sounds that surround you and allow yourself to be there with those sounds:
    - Is a baby crying?
    - Do you hear a car horn honking?
    - Can you hear your co-workers typing away on their keyboards?
- Step 3: Take a deep breath to help yourself settle
- Step 4: Follow your breaths:
    - How does it feel to inhale the air?
    - What does it feel like as it fills up your chest and belly?
    - How relieving is it to feel yourself exhale?
    - Does the air feel warmer or colder?
- Step 5: Repeat steps 1-4 at least five times

This brain hack allows you to grasp that you have the power to interrupt thoughts that distract you with simple meditation that doesn't involve hours sitting uncomfortably in a weird yoga pose. All you must do is close your eyes for 30 seconds and focus on your breathing. Doesn't sound like it would make much of an impact, but do it a few times and you will discover the wonders of this very simple way to control your habit to ruminate.

Yoga and Rumination Relief

There are many forms of yoga to choose from, but they all end in the same result when it comes to reducing rumination. This is why yoga classes are offered within schools, hospitals, long-term care facilities, etc. all over the world. Yoga is an activity that is broadly accepted and recommended by many.

Whether you choose yoga methods that make your sweat bullets or ones that allow you to stretch and relax your insides, at the end of a session you should feel like your entire body took one big sigh of relief. Yoga can clear our minds as well as relax our muscles. People had said time and time again that practicing and performing yoga melts away the stress and worries they had when they first started their session.

Benefits of Yoga for Relieving Rumination

Unique form of meditation

Yoga forces us to concentrate, which means we must clear our minds to perform it correctly.

Great exercise

Yoga involves stretching and conforming to different kinds of shapes your body can handle and must be able to hold for a period of time. It tones your muscles and strengthens many parts of your body.

Turns off your stress responses

Proper yoga practices involve you performing deep breathing exercises and relaxation techniques. This is probably the most difficult part of mastering yoga.

Tunes into physical awareness

Yoga encourages the dismissal of any negative thoughts that may be racing around your mind. It makes you focus on your breathing as you fuel your body with the air from the outside world. Certain poses can only be performed when you rid your mind from the nonsense within it and target your focus towards all the muscles moving inside you to get yourself into those poses and stances.

Establishes the importance of breathing exercises

The core of yoga is referred to as "pranayama," also known as controlled methods of breathing. Effective breathing alone is a great method to use when coping with anxiety and depressive symptoms. These exercises allow one to dive deep within themselves and erase troubling feelings or thoughts that plague the mind. This allows one to think more clearly when it comes to problem-solving and absorbing whatever troubling them. Practice makes perfect when it comes to deep breathing. It is a great form of stress reduction and is encouraged to be used within your daily routine or when you need to take a step back and clear your mind.

Chapter 6: Daily Routines to Beat Rumination

Those that suffer from ruminating thoughts get stuck easily in a stressful situations or environments. Your brain gets caught up in a messy web that entraps you and leaves you thinking negatively and irrationally.

This means you have to find small ways to counteract these feelings that gang up on you. It is vital for you to have your own personalized anxiety routine to help you get untangled from the web of anxiety-fueled negativity.

What are rumination/anxiety routines?

Rumination and/or anxiety routines are daily routines, they are a form of self care. They assist in calming yourself down in any kind of situation that leaves you feeling physically, mentally or emotionally distressed and that have the power to bounce you back from the depths of your own thoughts.

We can't control our subconscious thoughts, those are the ones that just pop into our head without our permission. What we *can* do is control how we cope with those thoughts. When you have a system or a routine that you rely on, you can use that as support that is outside your head. That way you're fighting unwanted thoughts with actions instead of more thoughts.

Life runs smoother when you have a routine to quiet the little voices in your head. Many individuals choose very unhealthy habitual routines that push them back into a negative state. Such routines may even provoke symptoms of anxiety and make them experience rumination at a worsened rate.

These bad routines could be anything from drug use, both illegal and prescription, large consumption of alcohol or heavy smoking of cigarettes, etc. You get the picture. Creating a routine for yourself should not include things that will cause you greater harm in the long run. Those kinds of habits are only going to make your symptoms worse.

We are wired to detect any sort of negative energy that may cause us harm. Anxiety caused from rumination gets so bad. This is because our bodies do not know the difference between stressful triggers that are harmless to us versus actual, life-threatening aspects that may be sprung upon us – remember the evolution theory I discussed earlier.

Our bodies are made to react to protect ourselves. Therefore, being mentally prepared for the day that lies ahead of you is so crucial. It is important to back up our thoughts with an extra layer of positivity to promote a sense of safety and well-being. This is easier said than done, especially when life may not have been a very good friend to you as of late. But being able to mentally develop a positive sense of self is the first step in creating daily routines that help pave your way to a successful life to live and your future.

Steps to Positive Preparing

Write down your daily activities

- Did you wake up and start out calmly and easily without over stimulating yourself?
- Did you block out or let the outside world in?
- How did that feel?
- How did you feel when it was time to officially start the day ahead of you?
- What was your anxiety level before walking out the door?

Be aware of negativities that are ruling your mental self

People tend to believe that they just do not have the time to spare to get everything they need to get done completed. We always tell ourselves we do not have enough time. We also claim that we should put duties and deadlines before the needs of those in our lives. Also, we claim that particular things can just not wait. STOP. You are putting yourself in more frenzy than you realize!

If you do not have time, MAKE some. Think about getting up twenty to thirty minutes earlier in the morning. If you always put duties and/or other people before yourself, you are never going to get anywhere. Ensure that you are doing things for YOU too.

I learned the hard way that you cannot fill the cups of others when your pot is empty. Advances in technology have far exceeded our expectations and have many great benefits. But technology also tends to directly rule our lives. We constantly feel the need to check emails, to see who or how many followers liked our Facebook status, etc. Give yourself time to breathe without the distraction of your phone, computer, television, etc. Take in the world around you as it is.

Take back control

You are in control of your own life, even if you don't feel like it some days. Do not let errands, other individuals, or other aspects of everyday living put a leash on you and drag you around.

If your life is a car, *you* are the driver – never forget this. We often get bombarded with life's demands and forget that we are the ones in control. If your boss is always getting you down, start looking for a new job. If your relationship is falling apart, seek relationship therapy or read books on healthy relationships.

This may sound like I am oversimplifying but the truth is that when you get out of your head and start *taking action* it's a lot easier to stop thinking. Instead of thinking about what's bothering you, start actively trying to fix it.

Positive Habits to Incorporate into Your Routine

Suffering from the side effects of constant rumination can mean the difference of getting out of bed with hope and struggling to make it from under your sheets. Daily routines are crucial to a happier way of living, even for people that have their anxiety and ruminations under control.

Think about it this way, you do have a routine whether you've consciously made one or not. If your morning routine involves dragging yourself out of bed after snoozing for an hour, rushing to get out the house and showing up for work late *again* then that *is* your routine. It's not a healthy one though. It's better to consciously create your routine so that it works for you instead of against you.

Routines are responsible for setting the tone of the whole rest of the day, which means morning routines make the biggest impact. Being able to recognize when negative patterns of thought begin to enter the mind gives you the ability to stomp them out.

Healthy routines are full of ways that help you to focus on reducing stress. This is the main cause of rumination that leads to anxiety in the first place. Daily routines are stabilizers to the mind. They provide us with the confidence boost we need to kick-start positive emotions. These emotions assist us in feeling like we are unmistakably in control of ourselves, our thoughts and our course of actions throughout each day.

With the right amount of inspiration, the first few days of adding a new routine to your life can be exciting. You know you are making a positive change that will help you to feel better about yourself and the life you live.

However, self-care routines can be a hard thing to manage and utilize on a regular basis once the newness of acting upon it wears off. Anxiety can leave some sufferers so dismayed by negative thoughts. This can get to the extent that they want nothing more than to do away with anything that resonates positive energy. But this is the exact opposite of fighting for yourself and your happiness. Everyone has their bad days, and you are allowed to have them too. Just remember how important it is to not stay stuck in them for long periods of time.

Developing and executing specific daily routines that you are comfortable with gives you a step by step plan. This plan keeps you prepared for situations or other anxiety triggers from leaping out and mugging you of your happiness. Routines, kind of like exercise, are things we practice daily to keep us in shape, but self care routines keep our minds in check.

Benefits of Everyday Routines

Creating and sticking to a morning routine every morning is not only a big part in relieving rumination. It also boosts productivity, brings out your inner positivity, helps you to develop and successfully sustain good relationships, as well as it just being a big reducer of negativities in many aspects of life in general.

Routines have been shown to be the best strategy for reducing stress and relieving those pesky symptoms of rumination. It is also a great way to keep you consciously aware as well as more grounded throughout the day. Many who were once stubborn were surprised at how much better they felt when they added healthy habits to their habitual routine(s). Anxiety levels dropped, and levels of confidence and happiness substantially rose. Routines can reduce your anxiety by as much as 60 percent!

The remainder of this chapter is full of easy to implement daily routines that if incorporated into your own anxious life, can assist you in building a new foundation that you can confidently stand upon and greet every day with a smile of motivation.

Healthy Habits for a Better Daily Routine

Wake up earlier

When you have plenty of time to get up and get ready for the day, your stress levels are decreased dramatically. If there is adrenaline constantly pumping throughout your body as you rush to the door, that feeling will be with you for much of the remainder of the day. This leaves you feeling on edge and never quite in a calm state of mind.

Stop looking at me with those eyes. If you're not a morning person, I know that "waking up earlier" is kind of the same as saying "just make more money" – easier said than done.

I struggled so hard with waking up early for many years. I tried putting my phone on my dresser so that I had to get up to turn off the alarm – it didn't work. I tried setting only one alarm at the time I had to get up, instead of five alarms going off every ten minutes – it didn't work. I tried using one of those sun lamps that gradually gets brighter in the morning– you guessed it, it didn't work!

What ended up working after countless attempts was the five minute strategy. Every day I would wake up five minutes earlier. I would set my alarm for 7am and then snooze until 8am. Then the next day, I would snooze until 7:55am. I did this until I could wake up at the first alarm – 7am and then kept doing this until I naturally woke up at 6am every morning.

The point I'm trying to make here is that if something doesn't work, keep trying. There is no one size fits all or this book would be one sentence long. Take the goals presented in this book and figure out strategies to achieve those goals that work for you.

Make the bed

Sounds silly, but the simple act of making your bed is more powerful than you think. Completing this task helps in building the momentum you need to get ready for the day, and it gives you a small positive boost of energy. Having your bed made is at least one great task you managed to complete that day, even if your ruminating thoughts keep you from completing nothing else.

Meditate

As discussed, meditation has countless benefits and is a great part of your morning routine.

Enjoy a cold shower

Yes, cold showers sound completely awful to many people, including me. However, it has been proven that getting in an ice-cold shower can lead to a great amount of benefits.

Cold exposure, also known as cold shower therapy, is nothing new. Our ancestors utilized it as a remedy to treat mental ailments like depression and anxiety. This method allows adequate circulation throughout the body and tones the skin.

The cold feeling on our body turns on a positive response throughout our system. It accelerates our body's way of repairing cells, which reduces inflammation and pain and speeds up our metabolic processes.

Studies have shown that cold showers stimulate the cerculeous in the brain, referred to by scientists as 'the blue spot.' This part of the mind excretes the hormones needs to alleviate us from symptoms of negative mental disorders.

This does not mean you must withstand cold water for ten minutes or more. Stand under the cold water for just two to three minutes, then proceed to take your hot shower. Just ensure that you again turn the water to cold at the end of your shower before jumping out. This helps in the circulation of blood and leads to your muscles contracting, ridding your body of toxins.

Write it out

Try writing out 'morning pages' in a notebook. These serve as a way to jot out anything that is troubling my mind, as well as any other random thoughts that pop up during those 5 to 15 minutes I sit down to write.

When you can write down all those mad, sad, angry, and confusing thoughts on paper, you can then get through the day with a clearer state of mind. Writing is a powerful tool that has substantial benefits when you truly incorporate it into your daily routines. They do not just have to be "morning" pages. You should jot down anything of such at night before bedtime as well. Call them 'bedtime pages' if that suits your fancy.

Practice daily gratitude

In the spirit of writing your thoughts and feeling out, I highly recommend keeping another notebook or journal that is dedicated solely to the things you are grateful for. While morning and/or bedtime pages are for the things that bother and plague you, a 'gratitude pages' are meant to be positive.

Writing the things that you are thankful for every day can help you to see your world in a different light. The key here is diversity in what you write out. This allows you to seek out the smaller aspects of your life that you may be unconsciously blind to. Think of things that you would greatly miss if they were to disappear or no longer be present. The three areas that I challenge you to look deeper into are the following:

- **Things you may not think about:**

    o   Ability to walk, run, exercise, etc.
    o   Running water
    o   Heat and air conditioning

- **Small things that make up your everyday life:**

  - The sound of silence
  - The cool side of your pillow
  - The wind brushing across your face
  - The warmth of a newly poured cup of coffee

- **People:**
  - Anyone important to you that you are grateful for each day of your life. This will help you to realize what life may be like without those people residing in it.

    - This could be your romantic partner
    - a loyal friend
    - a kind co-worker
    - a stranger you conversed with at the store
    - Etc.

Write out your daily "morning trio"

Many people find a sort of energetic reboot when they choose to write out affirmations on paper. <u>Seeing is</u>

believing and having them written out to visually see makes a world of difference when it comes to executing them.

To be able to start out the day on a positive note, it is a great step to jot down what you are looking forward to that day. This tells our brains to look up, think up, and be bright. This helps in relieving anxiety symptoms.

Instead of ruminating to the point that you do not wish to participate in the day at all, this gives you a boost to get through the other days' activities that will eventually bring you to the event you are looking forward to.

It is good practice, especially when it comes to putting a stop to those negative, anxious-fueled thoughts and feelings, to write down what intentions you have for the day that lies ahead. They can be as corny as you wish if they mean something to you. Examples are *"I will be consciously present today"* or *"I shall choose to seek out the beauty behind everything that happens to me today."*

Prioritize crucial daily tasks

Being prepared and having a plan to successfully triumph your days' most important missions eases your mind so that you can develop a clear path of action in achieving your goals. I know I have mentioned writing a lot, but like I said before, it is a powerful tool that has personally changed my life entirely.

Every morning, our brains are ready to go and on high alert. So, it is good to have a well-thought-out and detailed plan of action to take on the day ahead of you.

Write down at least three to five of the most important tasks that you must get done or at least start that day. Focus on the ones that stress you out just thinking about them. Then, ask yourself the following questions about the tasks you have jotted out so that you can prioritize them accordingly:

- Which tasks will help me inch closer to achieving my main goal?
- What task do I have the most fearful anxious thoughts about?
- Which tasks have the potential to cancel out others if done successfully?

Spend least 90 minutes accomplishing your daily priorities

Once you have narrowed down your top priorities to accomplish for the day, set aside at least an hour and a half of time to focus just on that task. It is vital to target your main goals during the morning hours because we are the most productive during the first three to four hours of the day.

Other Routine Strategies

Listen to positive, uplifting music

As human beings, we not only beat to the rhythm of our own inner drums, but we tend to be more upbeat when listening to relaxing and uplifting tunes. Everyone likes music!

Create a playlist that suits you that you can play throughout your routine when you get up to conquer the day. Make your alarm tone on your phone a good song to wake up to. You would be surprised at what a difference this effortless step takes! Whatever gives you that boost of energy, add it! Whether you enjoy more relaxed tones such as natural sounds such as the wind blowing or birds chirping or you like other music, listen intently to the variety of tones, what instruments are being utilized to make up the song and the lyrics if there are any.

Spend time with your furry friend

It is beneficial to play with your pets for both parties! Pets are enjoyable creatures that inhabit our lives. Take your dog on a walk, play with your cat. Pets are known to help raise our dopamine and serotonin levels, which aids anxiety and depression that leads to rumination.

Pets are also a motivator to get out of bed, even when you really have no desire to do so. The initiative comes from having to feed, water and love them. So, adding them to your daily routine is a bonus for not only you but for your pet's well-being too!

Change your scenery

It is easy to feel trapped within the comfort of your own home when you are heavily ruminating and drowning in your thoughts. Even though our brains inform us to avoid social interactions at all costs, this is the last thing you should do.

- Go outside, take a walk
- Visit your favorite café and grab a coffee
- Go out with a friend

The longer you dwell in a space that sucks away your happiness, the worse and more overwhelmed you will feel. Interactions with the outside world can be enough to distract you from your mind's negative habits.

Routines are so important in alleviating rumination. Avoiding responsibilities can actually damage you mentally more than you realize. It is good to get your attention off the darkness of life that resides inside your head. It only makes your anxiety worse when you sit around and obsess over it.

Chapter 7: Controlling the Mind

Our minds are the command center for the way we feel, the way we view the world, and how we achieve everything we were meant to accomplish in this lifetime. However, our minds can be the one thing that holds us back from being successful individuals. So, how does one go about taking back control of their brain? Here are some suggestions.

Distract yourself

When you are feeling bogged down by your feelings, distract yourself with magazines, movies, or books or head to a busy street, park, or museum. Doing this forces you to take the aspects of life and the culture you are in, whether you like it or not. When you are mindfully involved in the outside world, your mind has a chance to recharge and pick another path.

Repeat a comforting affirmation

Pick a phase, affirmation, prayer, poem, or song that brings you comfort. Learn all the words and repeat this to yourself when ruminating thoughts begin to take over your mind and/or ruin your day.

Stop 'awfulizing' life

When you are constantly thinking that things are going to end up awful or catastrophic, you are always going to expect the worst. What way is that to live? It's not.

Instead, turn your assumptions from hysterical to objective by writing out your fears and the worst things that could potentially occur. Then write down three or more positive outcomes. Look at everything you wrote. See which ones are more realistic? This helps you to be measured and bring your mind back to Earth.

Count your blessings

The more grateful you are about even the smallest things in your life, the happier you are bound to be. I always tell others to count their blessings instead of sheep.

Visit people

If you find yourself ruminating in your thoughts, get together with a family member or friend that you haven't seen for a while. Make simple plans to get coffee or eat out. Those that know you well can respond sensitively or can do their best to make you laugh and feel better about life.

Get into gear

Motivate yourself and go out of your way to get more done than you think you can, more than you wish to, and more than you need to. Get at least 5 things completed instead of just 3. This makes you rush and get a little manic but in a good, motivational way.

Get physical

Perhaps it is time to give yoga or a round in the boxing ring a try. There are some that prefer to punch their feelings out, and there are others that like to stretch it out instead.

Ultimately, you want to do everything in your power to get out of your mind. You don't want to be spending ample amounts of time with the demons in your head.

How to Become the CEO Of Your Brain

We all have come into hard times when it comes to trying to take back control of the reigns that hold our mind. While being positive works for a while, for many, this is very temporary. However, with the following steps, you can truly become the king of your mind, your thoughts, and the way you feel day in and day out:

Step 1: Listen and acknowledge

Just as if you were the CEO of a company, you have to take the time to listen to those disgruntled employees and acknowledge what they are saying. Our minds are the same way; they are better able to let go and relax when they are heard and understood.

Be grateful and thank your mind for its contribution to your life:

- "Mind, thank you for reminding me that I may get fired if I don't work harder to make more sales."
- "I need to do my best with every opportunity presented to me in life."
- "I need to learn from my past, so I don't make the same mistakes again."

Step 2: Make peace with your mind

You will not always like what your big, beautiful brain conducts itself and the negativity it presents you can be rather irritating. However, you are stuck with the brain you got, and you can't trade it in for a newer model; but you can revamp it and make it better in an exuberate number of ways.

You need to accept that negative thoughts and feelings will always be there, and you can't control that, but you do have a say in how they interfere with your actions. You can choose to dwell or to rise above and move on with your life. You don't have to like the thoughts your brain digs up, but you can let them sit where they are as you conquer the world.

Step 3: Remember that thoughts are *just* thoughts

We can't "see" our minds, per say, for they are just a part of us and who we are. Essentially, we are "fused with our thoughts." This means they are stuck together in such a way that they make up who you are, which is why you should do your best to unconditionally accept them.

Our thoughts are mental, passing events that are influences by our moods, hunger, tiredness, physical health, hormones, sex, weather, what we learned as children, what we ate last night, what we watched on T.V., etc. They are essentially mental habits. Like any other habits, they are either healthy of unhealthy and take time to change.

Coach potatoes can't decide they can run a 5-mile marathon one day and succeed, so how does one think they can turn off their negative cycles of thought and feeling without effort and practice?

Step 4: Observe your mind

The old saying, "know thine enemy" is just as applicable when we talk about the relationship we have with our minds. Leaders spend time walking from office to office, getting to know their employees just like we need to devote time to our minds each day.

Time spent observing your feelings and thoughts is just as vital as daily exercise. Focusing your mind on the rhythms of your breath or the nature outside, it has a chance to wander, bringing up unsolved issues or expired worries. If these are left unchecked, they can easily pile up and make your spiral into worry and fear, even during peaceful moments.

Practicing mindfulness helps you to notice where your mind wanders to and gives you the ability to bring it back into focus, whether you are working, loving, walking, eating, breathing, etc. When you perform mindfulness techniques, you strengthen your ability to retrain your brain to know when it's going unchecked and bring it back to reality.

Step 5: Retrain to Rewire

"We are what we repeatedly do" is one of the truest sayings in the world when it comes to the topic of constant rumination. This means we also become what we repeatedly think as well. Our thinking patterns become etched into even the tiniest of neurons in our brain, connecting them together to make entrenched patterns. When certain connections are constantly repeated, those neurons transmit information into an interconnected sequence. When one thought is ignited, the rest of the sequence is then activated.

The autopilot may be great for planes and cars, but it isn't the best for functioning emotionally as a human being. Over time, you do have the chance to rewire the brain so that it is able to influence and shut off those rapid-firing sequences of negativity.

For instance, if you have fears of getting close to others or letting them into your life because of how you were treated as a kid, you have to learn to love again. To do this, you will be required to be aware of the entire sequence of negativity and how it biases your perceptions.

Step 6: Practice self-compassion

We cannot change the reactions and feelings that our minds and bodies create, but we do have the potential to change how we respond to these feelings. Many of us were taught from an early age to hide vulnerable feelings. Realistically, however, being vulnerable can be a better source of confidence and strength than we realize when managed properly.

When we judge our own feelings, we lose touch with the benefits that can occur from them. Feelings are valuable and provide information about our reactions to certain life events. They inform us about what is meaningful and important to us personally. Instead of criticizing yourself, you should learn new methods of supporting yourself. Seek out both inner and outer opportunities that bring your comfort and joy, such as happy memories, nature in all its beauty, your creativity, etc.

To be a great CEO of your mind, you must be willing to listen, acknowledge, realize, and make peace with what your mind is. Remind yourself that you do have the ability to retrain your brain to a certain extent. In doing this, your mind will greet you with a lifetime of positive loyalty and service.

Chapter 8: Creative Outlets

In everyday life, especially at work, we don't turn to any type of creative outlets to cope with stress and thoughts that ruminate and plague us. A huge part of being happy is being creative and having hobbies and activities that help us to express ourselves and be different from the rest of the world.

Even if you have never thought of yourself as an artsy person, the idea here is to not create the next Van Gough but to express yourself and create something from what you are feeling.

Write

Type or physically write down your thoughts about anything you wish, from thoughts that upset you to happy emotions. Research shows that writing out negative experiences for just 15 minutes per day can help people feel much better. You can keep your writings private or show them to trusted people. Who knows; perhaps your pain can become a gain when shown to others.

Creative writing

Making up your own tale is very relaxing, and as an author, your story can go in whatever path you feel at the time. Here are a few writing prompts to get you started:

- Start with this sentence: *"The human mind is the scariest thing of all."*
- Create a fairy tale or story you have read from the perspective of the villain
- Imagine yourself as a child's imaginary friend that is fading away as they grow older.
- Her life changed once she learned that the monsters were protecting her.

Improvisation /Acting Classes

Take an acting or improv class to give you a reason to act silly and connect with others. Using your body is a great way to get out of your head and comedy/acting is an excellent way to learn how to stop taking things so seriously.

Sketch

Get yourself an art pad and some colored pencils and go to a favorite scenic spot or an art gallery and draw what you see.

Paint

Gather paints and brushes and make a mini-studio in the kitchen of your home. Pick a picture from a magazine or Pinterest and paint your own masterpiece.

Be musical

Did you use to play an instrument? If you still have it, pick it back up and take it up once again. You can also learn how to play instrument, learn how to sing, go to a karaoke night or experiment with making music digitally.

Take pictures

Dust off your camera or take your smartphone and snap pictures. I know I personally love tinkering around with photo editing to get my mind off things and it is a great excuse to get out of the house.

Make a homemade movie

With your phone or video camera, film your kids, your pet, your home, etc. Write your own script or go with the flow.

Try out new hobbies

- Antiques
- Archery
- Astrology
- Astronomy

- Beer tasting
- Birdwatching
- Bowling
- Boxing
- Breakdancing
- Ceramics and pottery
- Cheese tasting
- Coin collecting
- DJ-ing
- Drones
- Fishing or fly fishing
- Floristry
- Geology
- Guitar
- Hunting
- Investing
- Jewelry making
- Learn a new language
- Martial arts
- Needlepoint or knitting
- And <u>many more</u>!

Chapter 9: Continuing the Fight Against Rumination

We have an estimated 70,000 thoughts *per day,* which are 70,000 chances to build ourselves up or tear ourselves down. To continue the fight against the thoughts that cause us to ruminate, the last chapter will discuss some daily methods to keep negativity at bay.

Daily exercises

Give yourself the advice you would tell a friend

There's a very good chance that you are just critical of yourself and you are dragging yourself down by magnifying your mistakes. Talk to yourself in the same ways that you would speak to a trusted friend you care about.

Label your emotions

Most people dislike discussing their feelings or showing them. This is why many become distant from the way they feel, which makes it harder for them to recognize how they feel.

When you give yourself a chance to label how you are feeling you are acknowledging your emotional states of mind, which gives you a chance to consider how those feelings may affect your emotions and the ability to make sound decisions.

When you feel crummy about things in your personal life, or you are concerned about things happening at work, your emotions are inevitably going to spill over into other aspects of your life if you fail to be aware of them and control them when they begin to sprout.

Balance emotions with logic

Are you in a financial bondage? Are you experiencing a family dilemma? You are able to make better decisions when you can balance out your emotions with logic. When you have high-running emotions, you need to take the time to increase your rational train of thought. Create a list of the pros and cons of your situations you are at war over. Reading over that list will help you to take some of your emotions from your final decision and give you're the ability to make the best possible decisions for *you*.

Conclusion

I hope that the chapters of this book were able to provide you with the tools you need to begin living a much better, happier, and healthier life, both inside and out. We all deserve to know ways that we can pick ourselves up off the ground when life knocks us down.

Remember that the way to cure yourself of negative rumination is to start building positive roads. It should be a main goal of your life to always build positive roads whenever you have an opportunity and I hope this book gave you a number of road building techniques to try.

Finally, if you found this book useful in anyway, a review on Amazon is always appreciated!

FREE 10 Day Self Care Challenge

- Subscribe to my email list and get my 10 Day Self Care Challenge as a FREE bonus
- 10 Days of actionable tasks to help get you started on your self care journey.
- Download all 10 days in one PDF
- Clear your mind, feel happier
- Note: You will receive notifications for when my next eBook goes on FREE promo
- https://millennialships.lpages.co/rumination-optin/

Made in the USA
Las Vegas, NV
08 February 2021

17486079R00059